First Facts®

REALLY **SCARY** STUFF

SCARY PLACES

by Jim Whiting

Consultant:
Elizabeth Tucker
Professor of English
Binghamton University
Binghamton, New York

CAPSTONE PRESS
a capstone imprint

First Facts is published by Capstone Press,
151 Good Counsel Drive, P.O. Box 669, Mankato, Minnesota 56002.
www.capstonepub.com

Books published by Capstone Press are manufactured with paper
containing at least 10 percent post-consumer waste.

Library of Congress Cataloging-in-Publication Data
Whiting, Jim, 1951–
    Scary places / by Jim Whiting.
    p. cm. — (First Facts, really scary stuff)
    Includes bibliographical references and index.
    Summary: "Describes places that have been the location of mysterious events and explores
whether or not the events could have happened" — Provided by publisher.
    ISBN 978-1-4296-3970-5 (library binding)
    1. Haunted places — Juvenile literature. I. Title. II. Series.
BF1461.W486 2010
001.94 — dc22   2009023637

Editorial Credits
Jennifer Besel, editor; Alison Thiele, designer; Marcie Spence, media researcher;
    Eric Manske, production specialist

Photo Credits
Alamy/Clint Farlinger, 10; Alamy/Lee Foster, 14; The Art Archive/John Meek, 16; CORBIS/
Bettmann, 7, 11; CORBIS/epa, 21; Corrington Enterprises, 15; Fortean Picture Library, 8, 20;
Getty Images Inc./Time Life Pictures/Mansell, 12; Newscom, 18; Shutterstock/dundanim, 5;
Shutterstock/E.G. Pors, cover

**The legends and stories presented in this book may have different versions. The versions used
in this book are considered by researchers to be the most common telling of the event or story.**

Printed in the United States of America in North Mankato, Minnesota.
112010
005998R

TABLE OF CONTENTS

Go There, If You Dare.. 4

Waves of Mystery 6

A Creepy Cave 10

The Cursed Tomb 13

A Ghost in the Hotel 14

A Haunted Ship 17

Faces on the Floor 20

Glossary.. 22

Read More... 23

Internet Sites.. 23

Index.. 24

Go There, If You Dare

Mysterious events happen in places all around the world. Ships **vanish** in the Atlantic Ocean. Faces appear on a floor in Spain. No one knows why these things happen. Turn the page to learn about some very scary places . . . if you dare.

vanish — to disappear

Mysterious events often happen in dark, old places. Will the mysteries ever be solved?

WAVES OF MYSTERY

The Atlantic Ocean may hide a secret. Airplanes and ships disappear in an area called the Bermuda Triangle.

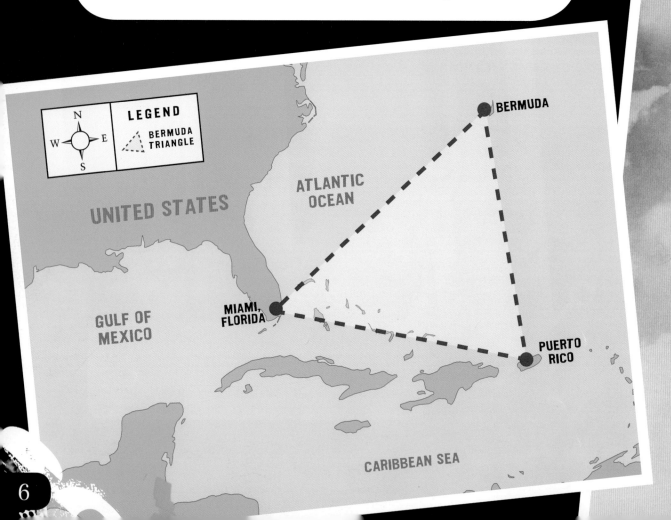

LEGEND

BERMUDA TRIANGLE

N
W • E
S

UNITED STATES

ATLANTIC OCEAN

BERMUDA

GULF OF MEXICO

MIAMI, FLORIDA

PUERTO RICO

CARIBBEAN SEA

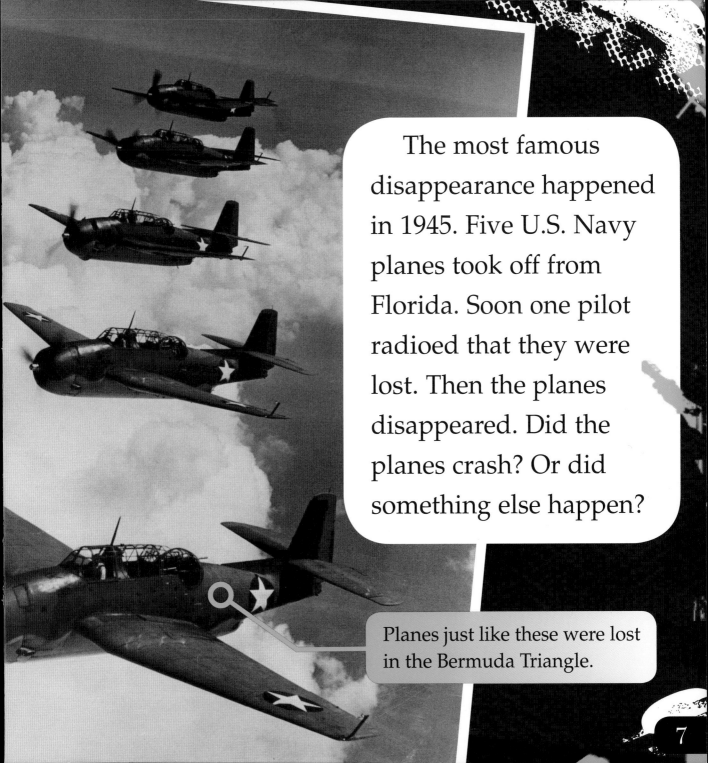

The most famous disappearance happened in 1945. Five U.S. Navy planes took off from Florida. Soon one pilot radioed that they were lost. Then the planes disappeared. Did the planes crash? Or did something else happen?

Planes just like these were lost in the Bermuda Triangle.

More than 100 planes and ships have vanished in the Bermuda Triangle. Some people believe space aliens captured vehicles going through the area. Others say the planes and ships sank.

FACT OR FICTION

Is Something Mysterious Taking Planes and Ships in the Bermuda Triangle?

Yes No wreckage or bodies were found from most of the vehicles that disappeared.

Yes No one saw the planes or ships disappear. Something could have taken them.

Yes Some travelers have reported that their cell phones and radios stop working inside the Triangle.

No Large, strong waves could quickly destroy wreckage. Sharks could have eaten the bodies.

No Strong storms or mechanical problems could have caused the planes and ships to sink.

No Many ships travel the area every day. Most never experience anything strange.

wreckage — the broken parts around the site of a crash

A CREEPY CAVE

Kentucky's Mammoth Cave may be one of the world's most haunted places. Visitors have reported more than 150 ghost sightings there.

haunt — to visit often, usually by ghosts

Do ghosts roam the dark Mammoth Cave?

Many people report seeing the ghost of Floyd Collins. Collins explored Mammoth Cave. One day, his leg was caught under a rock. He died before rescuers could save him. Many say Collins' ghost still roams the cave.

Floyd Collins died in the cave in 1925.

THE CURSED TOMB

King Tut was buried thousands of years ago in Egypt. In 1922, Howard Carter and Lord Carnarvon opened Tut's tomb. Soon after, Carnarvon died. Others who were at the tomb died a few years later. News reports said Tut's tomb was cursed. The curse killed anyone who disturbed the tomb. Could it be true?

tomb — a room for holding a dead body

cursed — affected by an evil spell

Howard Carter, left, explored Tut's tomb. Was the tomb cursed?

A GHOST IN THE HOTEL

You won't get much sleep at the Golden North Hotel in Skagway, Alaska. Three of the rooms are said to be haunted. Lights go on and off by themselves. Water mysteriously runs in empty, locked rooms.

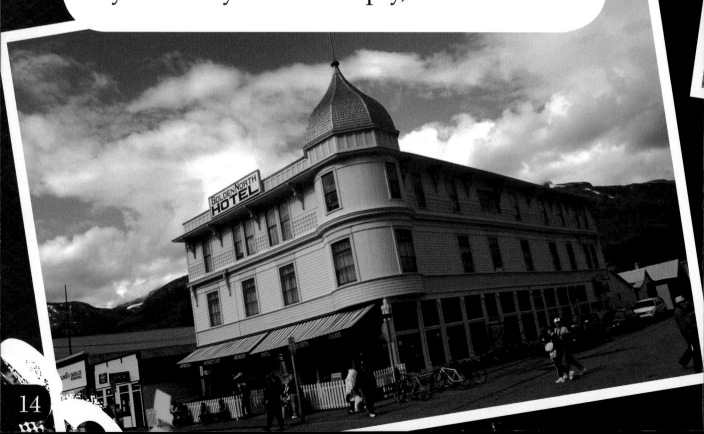

Room 24, where Mary may have died

Legend says that a woman named Mary died in one of the rooms. Mary died more than 100 years ago. Her ghost may still haunt the hotel.

legend — an old story that could be believable

A Haunted Ship

The *Queen Mary* could be one of the world's most haunted ships. This ship carried many passengers during peacetime and during war.

Many people died on the ship. A heavy door crushed two sailors. Two women drowned in the pool. Stories even say a cook was baked in an oven. Some people believe the ghosts of the dead haunt the ship.

the pool on the *Queen Mary*

Today the *Queen Mary* is a floating hotel in California. Some people claim to see wet footprints by the empty pool. Others say they've seen a girl searching for her mother. Are ghosts really there? Or do the guests just have good imaginations?

FACT OR FICTION

Is the *Queen Mary* Haunted?

Yes The owners of the ship closed room B340 to guests. There have been many reports of strange happenings there.

Yes Visitors say they have heard strange sounds. Researchers claim to have recorded ghosts talking.

Yes Researchers claim to have communicated with at least 150 different ghosts on the ship.

No Ghost stories didn't begin until the ship became a hotel. The owners may have created the stories to get people to visit.

No Strange noises could have natural causes. Pipes make sounds as they heat up and cool down.

No Most visitors to the *Queen Mary* never see or hear ghosts.

FACES ON THE FLOOR

In 1971, Maria Pereira discovered something scary. A face had appeared on the floor of her home in Belmez, Spain. Her husband replaced the floor. But more faces appeared. Scientists have studied these ghostly faces. They can't explain how they got there or why they won't go away.

The Pereira's house was built on an old graveyard. Are these faces caused by ghosts from the graveyard?

Creepy places like this are all over the world. But are these places really as scary as they sound?

GLOSSARY

cursed (KURSD) — affected by an evil spell

haunt (HAWNT) — to visit often, usually by ghosts

legend (LEJ-uhnd) — a story handed down from earlier times that could seem believable

tomb (TOOM) — a grave, room, or building for holding a dead body

vanish (VAN-ish) — to disappear suddenly

wreckage (REK-ij) — the broken parts or pieces around the site of a crash or explosion

READ MORE

Parvis, Sarah. *Haunted Hotels.* Scary Places. New York: Bearport, 2008.

Tourville, Amanda Doering. *King Tut's Tomb.* Ancient Egypt. Mankato, Minn.: Capstone Press, 2009.

Walker, Kathryn. *Mysteries of the Bermuda Triangle.* Unsolved! New York: Crabtree, 2009.

INTERNET SITES

FactHound offers a safe, fun way to find Internet sites related to this book. All of the sites on FactHound have been researched by our staff.

Here's all you do:

Visit *www.facthound.com*

FactHound will fetch the best sites for you!

INDEX

airplanes, 6, 7, 8, 9
Atlantic Ocean, 4, 6

Belmez, Spain, 4, 20
Bermuda Triangle, 6, 7, 8, 9

Carnarvon, Lord, 13
Carter, Howard, 13
Collins, Floyd, 11
curses, 13

ghostly faces, 4, 20, 21
ghosts, 10, 11, 15, 18, 19,
        20, 21
Golden North Hotel, 14, 15

King Tut's tomb, 13

Mammoth Cave, 10, 11

Pereira, Maria, 20

Queen Mary, 17, 18, 19

ships, 4, 6, 8, 9, 17, 19
Skagway, Alaska, 14